All In

by Tamara Ackerman

Introduction

All In is the ultimate resource guide for the salon and spa industry with words of wisdom, empowering tools, and helpful resources you can implement to help you achieve the level of success you desire.

"All in" is the process of putting all of your energy and enthusiasm into doing what it takes to be successful in your business or career.

To maximize your business success, your commitment depends on you being *all in*!

Work Smarter, Not Harder

When you're starting out, performing new services, practicing new techniques, and developing good work habits take time. The key to mastering anything is to do it again and again while making adjustments along the way. With time and practice, you will perfect your technique and reduce the time it takes to perform it.

Efficiency is the key. Once you become efficient in performing your technique, you no longer need as much time as you did originally to do that service. As you get better and better, you need less time. The secret is to stop allowing yourself as much time. Shave 5 minutes off the amount of time you give yourself. A few days later, shave off 5 more minutes. Keep doing this until you reach the ideal amount of time for the technique. In that shortened amount of time, you will complete the service or technique with the same amount of quality, and you'll have more energy for the next service. When you have more energy, you become more efficient. This allows you to work smarter, not harder.

Consider two technicians who do eyelash extensions. Jennifer is still learning and perfecting her eyelash extension application. Jennifer knows that each guest is different when it comes to how many lashes she will need to apply. Therefore, the time it takes to be efficient is different for each guest. Jennifer starts out by putting in 10-hour days; for 9 of those hours, Jennifer works on her guests, and she uses the other hour for two half-hour breaks. Because Jennifer is still learning how to be more efficient, she schedules 3 hours for a full lash application for each guest. In a 10-hour workday, Jennifer is only able to take three guests. Because customers pay $80 for an eyelash extension, she has a service total of $240.

Caitlin has been perfecting her eyelash extension technique and has become more efficient. She works an 8-hour workday with a half-hour break. It takes her 1 1/2 hours for each full application and an hour for a fill application. She can schedule 4 full applications and a fill application in her 8-hour shift; plus she can take a half-hour lunch break and spend a half-hour on marketing her services or doing other business tasks. She has worked 2 hours less than Jennifer and made $370 (she charges $80 for a full application and $50 for a fill).

Caitlin has accomplished more in her business and made quite a bit more money in an 8-hour workday compared with Jennifer's 10-hour workday. This is a perfect example of working smarter, not harder. Caitlin will have more energy at the end of her workday and has mastered how to be efficient.

Keeping Your Word

Faithfulness: to be reliable, trusted, or believed to be loyal and true to one's word, promises, and vows.

Stop and think about the true meaning of faithfulness for a few minutes. Break down each word in the definition and be honest with yourself in assessing how faithful you are.

If you could grade yourself on a scale of 1–5, 1 being weak, and 5 being very strong, how would you score your level of faithfulness?

How faithful are you to your guests?

How faithful are you to your team and to your boss? Do you remain loyal to them?

Ask yourself, am I loyal? Am I reliable, or do I come in late or call in sick often? Do I keep my word, or do I move guests' appointment times around? If you tell your boss you will be in on time or tell a guest that you will do her hair for her wedding but you don't follow through, then you are not keeping your word. This affects the level of your faithfulness.

If you are a salon owner or manager and you tell your team you will make changes to improve the work environment or you will put a stop to gossip in the salon or you will market differently to increase clientele but you don't do any of these things, then you fail to keep your word. Your level of faithfulness is affected, as is the trust your team has in you.

Many individuals, whether technician, owner, or manager, make comments to guests about how they should be loyal to them and see only them for hair, nail, or body services. *Really?* Well, I have news for you. Your guests are going to leave you if you do not stay on top of your game and stay loyal to them.

What are you doing to always give your guests 100 percent of your best efforts? "Best efforts" extends beyond your technical skills. It includes customer service, such as being on time for guests' appointments and not moving them around all the time because something came up. It also means giving them the look you committed to giving them, which means you need to continually educate yourself so you can be loyal to them.

Sometimes an owner or manager thinks her employees or staff should not go to another salon, or even open their own, because she built that team member. *What?* If you want loyalty from your team and you do not want them to leave, you must keep your word and be loyal to your team. Always give 100 percent because 95 percent is not going to cut it. People who want what's in that missing 5 percent will slip through your doors when you're not paying attention. Those who leave may be the employees you cannot afford to lose; usually these are your loyal ones. If being loyal is a core value to them, then they will not tolerate you not being loyal to them. Eventually, you will lose them. In addition to being loyal, you need to invest in your own education so you can be a better leader and be more motivated for your team.
How do you support and encourage positive energy at work? Do you create positive energy for yourself before heading into work? How about when you get there? If you have a team member with extra energy and she is beaming happiness and spreading it around, do you make fun of her for being too happy for your liking? I hope not! Get on board with liking, loving, and enjoying what you do.

The choice to be positive or negative is yours. If you don't choose to be onboard the happy train, you create a culture where people are uncomfortable or do not want to be. That will hurt your business. Your guests and team members want to be around people who fill them up, not empty them.

Your appearance also affects the culture you create for your guests. Dress for Success.

Make sure your hair, makeup, and nails look good at all times. A professional image sends a message that you care about how you look, which in turn tells your guests that you care how they look and will put time into making sure they look and feel good.

Salon Etiquette

Salon etiquette is an important part of your business. It can reflect on how you run your business and potentially be harmful if it offends a guest or makes them uncomfortable in any way. When considering the etiquette your guests experience in your salon, examine the areas listed below. When you follow these concepts and provide your guests with proper etiquette, you will increase client retention and gain more referrals.

- **Customer service:** A positive attitude and the first impression your guest has of you create an impact. Make them count.

- **Ambiance:** Make your space welcoming for your guest. Include a sensory experience (sight, touch, smell, hear, and taste).

- **Noise:** Keep noise to a minimum. If the salon is very busy and louder than usual, distract your guest with a soft-spoken conversation and a relaxing experience through touch, such as a scalp massage or a warm neck wrap. Keep your guest at ease.

- **Scent:** Make sure the salon is well ventilated and your perfume or cologne is not too strong. Using lavender or other aromatherapy scents adds to the guest's experience.

- **Cleanliness:** Make sure your space and your environment are clean so your guests are comfortable and feel good in their surroundings.

- **Application**: Be precise with your application process. You do not want to get unwanted product on the client's hair, skin, clothes, or accessories.

- **Personal hygiene:** Make sure your perfume or cologne isn't overwhelming and you don't have any body odor.

- **Conversation:** Be friendly. Focus the conversation on your guest, and avoid disruptions from others.

- **Language:** Swearing can be offensive to guests—not only to those in your chair but to those sitting nearby as well.

- **Body language:** Gestures, such as eye rolling, negative gestures, or head shaking, can also offend guests. It doesn't matter who your body language is aimed at; inappropriate body language can result in guests not returning. Guests watch how you treat them and the other people—staff and clients—in your salon.

- **Professionalism:** Dress professionally, act professionally, and speak professionally at all times (even to your coworkers).

Culture

What do you want your salon or spa's culture to be like from a client's perspective? How about for you or your team members to work in? The culture you create has a huge effect on how your team members and guests perceive the environment.

Do you walk into the salon at the beginning of your day carrying all of your emotions with you? Are you tense after finishing a phone call on the way in that didn't go well? If so, your team members and guests can feel your harried vibe, which contributes to the culture in the salon. It is crucial that you leave any problems and negativity at the door when you go to work. Every day as you walk into your salon, choose whether you are going to make a positive or a negative contribution to the culture.

What do you do if another team member is contributing negatively to the culture? Do you empathize or sympathize with them, or do you remind them to leave their problems and negativity at the door? The more you empathize or sympathize with another team member on a negative topic—whether they have brought it into the salon or they have been part of it at work—the more you encourage and contribute to the negative culture. Any unwanted energy should always be removed, not stirred or nurtured.

Handling Conflict Without Disrupting the Culture

Conflicts will occur between individuals in your salon, and how you handle the conflict can make all the difference. Some examples of conflicts that can occur are; a guest who is unhappy with their product or service, a disagreement between a manager and a staff member, or even a difference of opinion between coworkers. If you are in the middle of a conflict between other individuals, or you happen to be in a conflict with another individual yourself, here are some guidelines you can follow without disrupting the culture.

- Always remain calm.
- Do not place blame on others.
- Remain neutral.
- The guest is always right. Treat them with that mind-set.
- Respect others, even if you are not being treated respectfully by them. Set a good example.
- Create healthy boundaries.
- Do not gossip.
- Do not bring others into the conflict. Do your best to resolve it yourself. However, if the other person is being abusive in any way, get help.
- Apologize if necessary.
- Be kind.
- Move onto another task as soon as you can and stay positive.

Tips for Gaining New Clients

Every business, no matter how new or how established, needs to find clients. Even if you have a long list of loyal clients, they won't be around forever. Some of them may move away; others may get too sick to come in for your services. You need to keep your name in the public eye so you can maintain or grow your clientele.

Networking is a very powerful tool you can use to gain new clients. There are several ways to network.

- **Get involved with a networking group or a chamber of commerce group.** These types of groups encourage their members to develop relationships with each other, and they usually let you spread the word about the services and products you offer. My business grew 20 percent from just one business-to-business networking group alone.

- **Join a local community group.** For example, if you work downtown, join the downtown business group that supports the community and helps other businesses grow. You will meet local business owners and their teams, and you might even find some great businesses to collaborate and cross-promote with.

- **Have a booth at a local expo or sponsor a nonprofit organization's fundraiser.** Organizers of local expos are eager to have new businesses have a booth at their event. Nonprofit groups are always looking for businesses to underwrite the cost of their charity events. These types of events are a great way to get your name out and meet people; to introduce potential clients to your salon and services; and to give back to the community.

Marketing is a must. You are sure to gain new clients if you market yourself or your business. Popular and effective marketing methods include posting to social media, creating e-marketing, handing out literature on your services and products, offering specials, and providing valuable education. You must have a strong marketing plan and maintain it for it to succeed.

- **Take full advantage of social media.** Facebook, Twitter, LinkedIn, and Google Plus are great resources. Use them to spread the word about your services or products. One of the best things about social media is that it's free.

- **Create e-marketing newsletters.** You can include special offers or an article that pertains to your current clients or guests. You can gain new clients by asking your current guests to pass the e-newsletter on to people they know, which generates a lot of (free!) publicity for your business. To increase the likelihood that your clients will forward your e-newsletter, hold a contest. If a current guest passes it along to someone they know who comes in for a service, their name gets entered into a drawing. You could offer a discounted or free service or product, or you could offer something from another local business as a cross-promotion. Develop a tracking system as proof that your current clients passed the e-newsletter along; you can potentially gain new client information this way as well.

- **Post and hand out literature about your business to local networking groups or community groups you are part of.** Create a flier or brochure about your referral program, an upcoming special on services or products, or an event you are hosting. Encourage your guests to share your information with people they know; reward them with an incentive if someone books a service and uses their name.

Providing a top-notch customer service experience is a natural way to get your current guests or clients to spread the word about you. When you impress a new guest or client with your customer service, they are highly likely to return. They might also tell people they know about you as well, especially when they receive compliments about how great they look.

- **Wow your guests by treating them well when they are in your salon.** Go beyond the basics by offering them water, hanging up their coat, and providing an inviting environment.

- **Make everything about them.** Keep your conversation about your guest or information that pertains to their service or product. They came to your salon because they wanted or needed something from you.

- **Be consistent.** Consistency is the key to retention, so make every customer service experience consistently great. You don't want to do all the work of getting a new client and then lose them due to inconsistency.

Communications Checklist

1. Ask questions about your client's hair: What do you like and not like about your hair? What shampoo are you using? How is it working for you? Ask the same questions about their conditioner and styling products.

2. Repeat what they have told you about their likes and what you are doing so you are clear on both ends.

3. Let the client know that you will be educating them on the issues they have been having, and ask their permission to do so. Explain what tools, techniques, and products you are using on them and why.

4. Let the client talk about herself. Ask about her hobbies, find common interests, discuss current events, or talk about community activities.

5. Avoid talking about religion and politics. Avoid negativity, gossip, and pessimism.

6. Educate the client on the maintenance of her look, and let her know when she needs to be seen again to maintain her look.

7. At the end of the service, show her the products you used and tell her she can choose what she needs to take with her.

8. Remind her of the maintenance appointment and ask which week fits her schedule. Example: "In four to five weeks, you will start to lose your color and/or the shape of your haircut. Does four or five weeks work best to come back for a maintenance appointment?" *Then book it!*

Open Hours of Opportunity

Most technicians have some open hours each week when they are available to take clients but have not booked anyone to fill that time. These open hours give you the perfect opportunity to work on your business. The following is a beneficial list created to help you maximize your productivity and business growth.

- Develop marketing promotions. For example, pre booking incentives, specials.

- Create marketing tools for referrals. For example, referral cards, drawings.

- Look up a new color or haircut in a magazine and visualize how you would create it.

- Make follow-up phone calls to new clients or clients who received a new look. Do this within 24 to 48 hours of seeing them.

- Send out thank-you cards or email new clients and/or clients who have referred someone to you.

- Send birthday cards or emails to clients.

- Plan to do something in the community and create marketing pieces to distribute to help grow your business. For example, referral cards, drawings, specials.

- Send out a card with a special offer in it to clients whom you have not seen in a while.

- Put together a direct mailing to potential clients in the area with a special incentive.

- Create a menu of mini-services that your clients can have done either after their appointment or while their color is processing.

- Compliment three team members. This will help you maintain a positive attitude and culture in your business.

The more you do for your guests to make them feel special, not only when they are in your salon but also when they are away from you, the more likely they will remain loyal to you. This kind of treatment results in word-of-mouth referrals. Clients who are extremely pleased with how you treat them will tell all of their family members and friends about their experience. You can't buy this type of marketing!

Habit

Habit: a settled or regular tendency or practice, especially one that is hard to give up.

Habits are both easy to form and hard to break. What makes a good habit a good habit in our industry? What makes a bad habit a really bad habit?

A lot of it begins with your vision of what your business morals and values are like, followed by how you practice them.

For example, when you first start in the industry, you tend to follow certain steps or systems you learned in school or from a certain leader or educator. In time and after gaining some experience, you tend to take shortcuts or create your own steps. Sometimes they better your business or customer service experience, and you create new habits as a result. In other situations, you create new steps or take shortcuts because of time constraints or laziness. These can turn into bad habits. At some point, these bad habits affect the level of service your guests receive on both a technical and customer service level.

So how do you hold yourself accountable and keep from slipping into bad habits? Surrounding yourself with strong leaders and good role models is a good start. However, it is your responsibility to make sure your actions are what they should be, so don't blame your leader or co-workers for the habits you have created. Books and seminars that focus on time management, motivation, and self-help can help you grow both professionally and personally and will help you hold yourself accountable for being the person you want to be in your business. As a result, you will stick to your good habits and create new ones along the way.

Sure, you can slip into bad habits. Circumstances in your personal life can affect you and get you off track, but when that happens, it is crucial to not let the bad habits invade your professional practice; get help to ensure they won't leak into your business.

What if bad habits do start to slip into your business? First, recognize the habit and be honest with yourself. Then get out of it immediately. Seek help from a mentor or a leader. Take action and get back on the path that leads to where you want to be.

Focal Point

Focal point; the central principle of your attention or activity.

Are you focused on your business? How about on your clients when they are with you? Where is your focal point? Is it on your business needs and where you are going with your business, or is it on what happened yesterday or last week or last year? What drives you to move forward? Do you have a vision of what that looks like? How about your clients? Are you focused on their needs and wants when they are in your chair, or are you focused on yourself, what's going on with you or your family, or a meeting you are going to have?

To be successful in your business, you need to stay focused and have a vision of what you want. This vision should include what your clients want from you. So ask yourself, where is my focal point? Be honest with yourself when answering these questions.

After you have established your focal point, determine what goals you need to be *all in* with your focus on your client or guest. After you have set those goals, create an action plan for each one. It takes action and lots of practice to break a habit or establish a new one. Check in daily on your goals and actions to see your progress. Make notes along the way to help yourself. Look back at your week as a whole and see the progress you have made. Then think about any work you need to tackle to move on to the next week of progress. Stay focused to succeed.

Daily Planning

Guest Name	Hours/ Minutes Available	Opportunity for Services	Action Plan	Added $ Amount

Weekly Planning

Goal	Mon.	Tues.	Wed.	Thurs.	Fri.	Sat.	Total
Service Total							
Average Service per Guest							
Retail Total							
Average Retail per Guest							
Total Guests							

Weekly Planning

Actual	Mon.	Tues.	Wed.	Thurs.	Fri.	Sat.	Total
Service Total							
Average Service per Guest							
Retail Total							
Average Retail per Guest							
Total Guests							

Weekly Planning

Increase + Decrease – $/#	Mon.	Tues.	Wed.	Thurs.	Fri.	Sat.	Total
Service Total							
Average Service per Guest							
Retail Total							
Average Retail per Guest							
Total Guests							

Monthly Planning

Goal	Week 1	Week 2	Week 3	Week 4	Week 5	Total
Service Total						
Average Service Total Per Guest						
Retail Total						
Average Retail Per Guest						
Total Guests						

Monthly Planning

Actual	Week 1	Week 2	Week 3	Week 4	Week 5	Total
Service Total						
Average Service per Guest						
Retail Total						
Average Retail per Guest						
Total Guests						

Monthly Planning

Increase + Decrease - $	Week 1	Week 2	Week 3	Week 4	Week 5	Total
Service Total						
Average Service Total Per Guest						
Retail Total						
Average Retail Per Guest						
Total Guests						

Photo Release Form

SALON/SPA NAME Website and Social Media Photo Release Form

SALON/SPA NAME occasionally uses photographs of clients for business marketing purposes on its website or other social media or in printed publications. I hereby grant SALON/SPA NAME, located at SALON/SPA ADDRESS, permission to use my photograph. Without any further consideration, I acknowledge that SALON/SPA NAME has the right to treat the photograph at its discretion. I also understand that once my image is posted on SALON/SPA URL, the image can and may be downloaded. Therefore, I agree to indemnify and hold SALON/SPA NAME harmless from any claims from any and all employees, owners, or independent contractors of SALON/SPA NAME.

GUEST NAME (PRINT)

NAME OF CHILD IF UNDER 18

GUEST EMAIL

GUEST PHONE

GUEST SIGNATURE

DATE

GUEST PARENT SIGNATURE (IF UNDER 18)

DATE

www.ingramcontent.com/pod-product-compliance
Lightning Source LLC
Chambersburg PA
CBHW042108110426
42742CB00033BA/27